THE COMPLETE VIETNAMESE *Cookbook*

MOUTHWATERING HOMEMADE RECIPES TO DISCOVER ONE OF THE BEST CUISINE IN THE WORLD

DERICK BELROSE

DERICK BELROSE

TABLE OF CONTENTS:

CHAPTER 1: VIETNAMESE RECIPES 7

    NOODLE SALAD WITH LEMONGRASS CHICKEN 8
    BEEF MEATBALLS 11
    VEGETARIAN PHO 13
    VIETNAMESE SANDWICH 16
    MAHO VIETNAMESE CHICKEN 18
    CHICKEN CABBAGE SALAD 20
    LEMONGRASS BEEF AND NOODLES 22
    FRENCH-VIETNAMESE SHAKING BEEF 25
    VIETNAMESE SPRING ROLL WITH PORK AND PRAWNS 28
    GRILLED LEMONGRASS CHICKEN 30
    VEGETARIAN CURRY SOUP 32
    LA SA GA SOUP 34
    SHRIMP SOUP 36
    PORK CHOPS 38
    SPRING ROLLS WITH DIPPING SAUCE 40
    SPRING ROLL PIZZA 42
    SPICY VIETNAMESE BEEF NOODLE SOUP 44
    NUOC CHAM 47
    GOLDEN CHICKEN WINGS 49
    BANH-MI 51
    BEEF AND RED CABBAGE BOWL 54
    BANH XEO 56
    EGGPLANT WITH SPICY SAUCE 59
    CARAMEL CHICKEN 61
    FRESH SPRING ROLLS 63
    VIETNAMESE SALAD ROLLS 65
    VIETNAMESE CHICKEN SALAD 67
    AROMATIC LAMB CHOPS 69
    PORK AND FIVE SPICE 71
    CARAMELIZED PORK 73
    PRAWN BANH MI 75
    VIETNAMESE STIR-FRY 77
    TOFU SALAD 79
    CHA GIO 81

SPICY VIETNAMESE PICKLED VEGETABLES	83
KABOCHA SQUASH SOUP	85
TABLE SAUCE	88
BEEF AND LETTUCE CURRY	89
CARAMEL COATED CATFISH	91
CHICKEN AND LONG-GRAIN RICE CONGEE	93
CAO LAU	95
SAIGON NOODLE SALAD	97
CARAMELIZED PORK BELLY	100
BRAISED GREEN BEANS WITH FRIED TOFU	102
LARB - LAOTIAN CHICKEN MINCE	105
VERMICELLI NOODLE BOWL	107
SALT-AND-PEPPER SHRIMP	110

© Copyright 2021 by Derick Belrose All rights reserved.

The following Book is reproduced below with the goal of providing information that is as accurate and reliable as possible. Regardless, purchasing this Book can be seen as consent to the fact that both the publisher and the author of this book are in no way experts on the topics discussed within and that any recommendations or suggestions that are made herein are for entertainment purposes only.

Professionals should be consulted as needed prior to undertaking any of the action endorsed herein.

This declaration is deemed fair and valid by both the American Bar Association and the Committee of Publishers Association and is legally binding throughout the United States.

Furthermore, the transmission, duplication, or reproduction of any of the following work including specific information will be considered an illegal act irrespective of if it is done electronically or in print. This extends to creating a secondary or tertiary copy of the work or a recorded copy and is only allowed with

the express written consent from the Publisher. All additional right reserved.

The information in the following pages is broadly considered a truthful and accurate account of facts and as such, any inattention, use,

or misuse of the information in question by the reader will render any resulting actions solely under their purview. There are no scenarios in which the publisher or the original author of this work can be in any fashion deemed liable for any hardship or damages that may befall them after undertaking information described herein.

Additionally, the information in the following pages is intended only for informational purposes and should thus be thought of as universal. As befitting its nature, it is presented without assurance regarding its prolonged validity or interim quality.

Trademarks that are mentioned are done without written consent and can in no way be considered an endorsement from the trademark holder.

CHAPTER 1:  VIETNAMESE RECIPES

NOODLE SALAD WITH LEMONGRASS CHICKEN

Prep:
20 mins
Cook:
10 mins
Additional:
3 hrs 45 mins
Total:
3 hrs 75 mins
Servings:
4
Yield:
4 servings

INGREDIENTS:

Lemongrass Chicken:

4 small skinless, boneless chicken breast halves

3 red chile peppers, stemmed

3 cloves garlic

2 stalks lemongrass, white parts only, finely sliced

4 tablespoons olive oil

2 tablespoons fish sauce

2 teaspoons sesame oil

2 teaspoons white sugar

1 teaspoon flaked sea salt

Vietnamese Sauce:

2 tablespoons white sugar
1 medium lemon, juiced
4 tablespoons water, or more as needed
2 tablespoons fish sauce
1 clove garlic, finely chopped
1 red chile pepper, finely chopped

Salad:

1 (8 ounce) package vermicelli rice noodles
½ cup baby lettuce, or to taste
½ cup julienned cucumber, or to taste
½ cup finely shredded carrot, or to taste
1 tablespoon finely chopped fresh cilantro, or to taste
1 tablespoon finely chopped fresh mint, or to taste

DIRECTIONS:

Step 1
Place chicken into a large zip-top freezer bag.

Step 2
Combine red chile peppers, garlic, lemongrass, olive oil, fish sauce, sesame oil, sugar, and salt in a food processor. Blend until finely chopped and combined. Pour marinade into the freezer bag, making sure chicken is well coated. Marinate in the refrigerator for at least 3 hours, or up to overnight.

Step 3
Remove chicken from the refrigerator 30 minutes before cooking to allow to come to room temperature.

Step 4
Heat a large cast iron or nonstick pan over medium-high heat. Cook chicken in batches until golden and caramelized on the outside and no longer pink in the centers, 7 to 10 minutes. Transfer chicken to a cutting board and cut into thick slices using a sharp knife.

Step 5
Place sugar in a medium bowl. Add lemon juice and stir to dissolve. Stir in water and fish sauce, followed by garlic and chile pepper. Allow flavors to settle, 5 to 10 minutes. Taste and adjust for seasoning; add more lemon juice or sugar as needed.

Step 6
Meanwhile, place noodles in a large bowl and cover with hot water. Set aside until noodles are softened, about 15 minutes.

Step 7
Place cooked noodles into serving bowls. Top with chicken, lettuce, cucumber, carrot, cilantro, mint, and sauce.

NUTRITION FACTS:

517 calories; protein 21.9g; carbohydrates 66.8g; fat 18.6g; cholesterol 48.2mg; sodium 1691.2mg.

BEEF MEATBALLS

Prep:
25 mins
Cook:
10 mins

INGREDIENTS:

Meatballs:

1 pound lean ground beef
1 cup finely chopped red onion
⅓ cup roughly chopped cilantro
4 cloves garlic, finely chopped
1 tablespoon peeled and finely chopped ginger
1 ½ tablespoons fish sauce
½ tablespoon honey
1 green chile pepper, chopped (Optional)
2 tablespoons canola oil

Sauce:

¼ cup hoisin sauce
2 tablespoons soy sauce
2 tablespoons water
1 tablespoon fish sauce
1 Thai chile pepper, finely chopped (Optional)

DIRECTIONS:

Step 1
Combine ground beef, onion, cilantro, garlic, ginger, fish sauce, honey, and chile pepper in a food processor and blend until mixed and minced. Transfer to a bowl.
Coat fingers and palms lightly with oil and scoop tablespoons of beef mixture to create equal-sized meatballs and place them on a plate.

Step 2
Heat oil in a deep pan over medium heat. Add meatballs; cover and cook 5 minutes. Turn meatballs over, cover pan, and cook until golden brown, about 5 minutes more.

Step 3
Combine hoisin sauce, soy sauce, water, fish sauce, and chile pepper in a bowl and serve with meatballs. Pour over meatballs or use as a dipping sauce.

NUTRITION FACTS:

363 calories; protein 24.8g; carbohydrates 17.5g; fat 21.5g; cholesterol 79.5mg; sodium 1466.8mg.

VEGETARIAN PHO

Prep:
30 mins
Cook:
1 hr 4 mins
Total:
1 hr 34 mins
Servings:
6
Yield:
6 bowls

INGREDIENTS:

Broth:

10 cups vegetable stock
1 onion, peeled and halved
¼ cup soy sauce
8 cloves garlic, coarsely chopped
2 (3 inch) cinnamon sticks
2 teaspoons ground ginger
2 pods star anise
2 bay leaves

Soup:

1 (16 ounce) package thin rice noodles (such as Thai Kitchen®)
2 tablespoons vegetable oil, or as needed
2 (14 ounce) packages firm tofu, drained and cut into 1/4-inch slices
8 ounces enoki mushrooms
4 scallions, thinly sliced
½ cup coarsely chopped cilantro
1 lime, cut into wedges
2 jalapeno peppers, sliced into rings
¼ cup mung bean sprouts
¼ cup Thai basil leaves, torn into bite-size pieces

DIRECTIONS:

Step 1
Place vegetable stock, onion, soy sauce, garlic, cinnamon sticks, ground ginger, star anise, and bay leaves in a large pot; bring to a boil. Reduce heat, cover, and simmer until flavors combine, 30 to 45 minutes. Remove solids with a slotted spoon and keep broth hot.

Step 2
Place noodles in a large bowl and cover with boiling water. Set aside until noodles are softened, 8 to 10 minutes. Drain and rinse thoroughly. Divide noodles among 6 serving bowls.

Step 3
Heat oil in a large skillet over medium-high heat until shimmering.
Add tofu in a single layer and fry, in batches, until golden brown, about 6 minutes per side.

Step 4
Simmer fried tofu and mushrooms in broth until heated through, about 5 minutes. Transfer to serving bowls. Top with scallions and cilantro. Ladle in hot broth.

Step 5
Serve lime wedges, jalapeno peppers, bean sprouts, and basil alongside for garnishing each bowl.

NUTRITION FACTS:

483 calories; protein 16.6g; carbohydrates 77.7g; fat 12.6g; sodium 1208.8mg.

VIETNAMESE SANDWICH

Prep:
10 mins
Cook:
5 mins
Total:
15 mins
Servings:
4
Yield:
4 sandwiches

INGREDIENTS:

4 boneless pork loin chops, cut 1/4 inch thick
4 (7 inch) French bread baguettes, split lengthwise
4 teaspoons mayonnaise, or to taste
1 ounce chile sauce with garlic
¼ cup fresh lime juice
1 small red onion, sliced into rings
1 medium cucumber, peeled and sliced lengthwise
2 tablespoons chopped fresh cilantro
salt and pepper to taste

DIRECTIONS:

Step 1
Preheat the oven's broiler. Place the pork chops on a broiling pan and set under the broiler. Cook for about 5 minutes, turning once, or until browned on each side.

Step 2
Open the French rolls and spread mayonnaise on the insides. Place one of the cooked pork chops into each roll. Spread chile sauce directly on the meat. Sprinkle with a little lime juice and top with slices of onion, cucumber, cilantro, salt and pepper. Finish with another quick drizzle of lime juice.

NUTRITION FACTS:

627 calories; protein 55.3g; carbohydrates 72.1g; fat 12.1g; cholesterol 123.8mg; sodium 908.1mg.

MAHO VIETNAMESE CHICKEN

Prep:
15 mins
Cook:
30 mins
Total:
45 mins
Servings:
4
Yield:
4 servings

INGREDIENTS:

2 cups uncooked white rice
4 cups water
3 tablespoons vegetable oil
2 cloves garlic, minced
3 skinless, boneless chicken breast halves - cut into bite-size pieces
2 tablespoons soy sauce, or to taste
½ cup dry-roasted, unsalted peanuts
4 large leaves of iceberg lettuce
1 (11 ounce) can mandarin oranges, drained

DIRECTIONS:

Step 1

Bring the rice and water to a boil in a saucepan over high heat. Reduce heat to medium-low, cover, and simmer until the rice is tender, and the liquid has been absorbed, 20 to 25 minutes. Let the rice stand, covered, while you finish the dish.

Step 2

Heat oil in a skillet over medium heat until shimmering, and cook and stir the garlic until fragrant, about 1 minute. Stir in the chicken, and cook and stir until seared and beginning to brown, about 5 minutes. Stir in soy sauce and peanuts, and cook and stir until the chicken is no longer pink inside, and the soy sauce has coated the chicken and peanuts, 5 more minutes. Remove the chicken mixture from the heat.

Step 3

Line 4 plates with lettuce leaves, and scoop 1 cup of cooked rice onto each leaf. Top with chicken-peanut mixture, and sprinkle each plate with mandarin orange slices.

NUTRITION FACTS:

693 calories; protein 31.4g; carbohydrates 91g; fat 22.2g; cholesterol 50.4mg; sodium 511.4mg.

CHICKEN CABBAGE SALAD

Prep:
15 mins
Additional:
4 hrs
Total:
4 hrs 15 mins
Servings:
6

INGREDIENTS:

1 head cabbage, cored and shredded
2 onions, halved and thinly sliced
2 cups shredded, cooked chicken breast
¼ cup olive oil
salt and pepper to taste
3 tablespoons lemon juice, or to taste

DIRECTIONS:

Step 1
In a large bowl, toss together the cabbage, onions, and chicken.
Toss with olive oil until everything is lightly coated. Season with salt and pepper
and continue to toss while adding lemon juice. Add enough lemon juice so that you can taste it in
every bite. Cover and refrigerate for at least 4 hours before serving. The longer it sets the more
the flavors mesh together and the better it tastes!

NUTRITION FACTS:

231 calories; protein 15.7g; carbohydrates 15.5g; fat 12.7g; cholesterol 35mg; sodium 66.1mg.

LEMONGRASS BEEF AND NOODLES

Prep:
20 mins
Cook:
35 mins
Additional:
30 mins
Total:
85 mins
Servings:
4
Yield:
4 servings

INGREDIENTS:

1 (8 ounce) package rice vermicelli noodles

⅓ cup minced lemongrass

2 tablespoons soy-based liquid seasoning

1 tablespoon dry sherry

1 tablespoon brown sugar

3 cloves garlic, minced

1 pound flank steak, thinly sliced

Sweetened Fish Sauce:

2 tablespoons warm water, or more as needed
2 tablespoons white sugar
½ medium lemon, juiced
¼ cup fish sauce
2 fresh red Thai chile peppers, minced
2 cloves garlic, finely minced
1 bunch Thai basil leaves, chopped, or to taste
1 bunch cilantro, chopped, or to taste
1 cup fresh bean sprouts, or to taste

DIRECTIONS:

Step 1
Bring a large pot of water to a boil. Add vermicelli noodles and cook until softened, 12 minutes. Drain noodles and rinse with cold water, stirring to separate the noodles. Set aside.

Step 2
Combine lemongrass, soy-based seasoning, sherry, brown sugar, and garlic in a bowl. Marinate flank steak in mixture, tossing evenly, and let sit for 30 minutes.

Step 3
Meanwhile, make sweetened fish sauce. Pour warm water into a small bowl; add sugar and lemon juice. Stir until sugar is dissolved. Stir in fish sauce,
Thai peppers, and garlic. Adjust to taste. Set aside.

Step 4

Heat a large skillet over medium-high heat. Cook sliced flank steak until firm but slightly pink in the center, 5 to 6 minutes per side. Arrange cooked vermicelli noodles in bowls for serving. Place steak on top and garnish with Thai basil leaves, cilantro, and bean sprouts. Pour sweetened fish sauce over the top.

NUTRITION FACTS:

411 calories; protein 24.7g; carbohydrates 58.3g; fat 9.8g; cholesterol 35.6mg; sodium 1214.8mg.

FRENCH-VIETNAMESE SHAKING BEEF

Prep:
30 mins
Cook:
5 mins
Additional:
1 hr
Total:
1 hr 35 mins
Servings:
6
Yield:
6 servings

INGREDIENTS:

Beef Marinade:

2 tablespoons minced garlic
2 tablespoons oyster sauce
1 ½ tablespoons white sugar
1 tablespoon fish sauce
1 tablespoon sesame oil
1 tablespoon soy sauce
1 teaspoon hoisin sauce
1 ½ pounds beef top sirloin, cut into 1-inch cubes

Vinaigrette:

½ cup rice vinegar
1 ½ tablespoons white sugar
1 ½ teaspoons salt
1 red onion, thinly sliced

Dipping Sauce:

1 lime, juiced
½ teaspoon salt
½ teaspoon ground black pepper
2 tablespoons cooking oil
2 bunches watercress, torn
2 tomatoes, thinly sliced

DIRECTIONS:

Step 1
Whisk garlic, oyster sauce, 1 1/2 tablespoons sugar, fish sauce, sesame oil, soy sauce, and hoisin sauce together in a bowl; add beef. Marinate beef in refrigerator for at least 1 hour.

Step 2
Whisk vinegar, 1 1/2 tablespoons sugar, and 1 1/2 teaspoons salt together in a bowl until vinaigrette is smooth; add onion. Refrigerate for 10 minutes to pickle the onion.

Step 3
Whisk lime juice, 1/2 teaspoon salt, and black pepper together in a bowl until dipping sauce is smooth. Transfer dipping sauce to ramekins.

Step 4

Heat cooking oil in a wok or large skillet over high heat until oil starts to smoke; add beef. Cook in a single layer until beef is seared, about 2 minutes. Cook and stir (or "shake") until beef reaches desired doneness, 2 to 4 minutes.

Step 5

Spread watercress onto a serving plate and top with tomatoes.
Drizzle vinaigrette over tomatoes and layer beef onto watercress; top with onion.
Serve dipping sauce on the side.

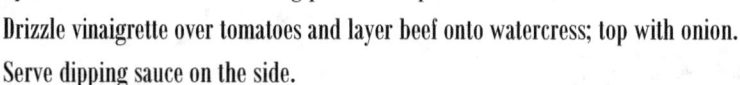

NUTRITION FACTS:

293 calories; protein 21.7g; carbohydrates 13.3g; fat 17.4g; cholesterol 60.5mg; sodium 1238.2mg.

VIETNAMESE SPRING ROLL WITH PORK AND PRAWNS

Prep:
45 mins
Cook:
10 mins
Total:
55 mins
Servings:
6
Yield:
6 servings

INGREDIENTS:

½ pound pork tenderloin, cut into thin strips
½ pound prawns, peeled and deveined
¼ pound rice vermicelli noodles
1 (12 ounce) package rice wrappers (such as Blue Dragon®)
1 bunch fresh cilantro, leaves picked from stems
5 spring onions, cut in half
¼ cup fresh mint leaves, or more to taste
¼ head romaine lettuce, cut into bite-size pieces

DIRECTIONS:

Step 1
Heat a skillet over medium heat; cook and stir pork in the hot skillet until cooked through, 5 to 7 minutes.

Step 2
Bring a pot of water to a boil; add prawns and cook until meat is pink. Drain water and slice prawns in half lengthwise.

Step 3
Fill a large pot with lightly salted water and bring to a rolling boil; stir in vermicelli and return to a boil. Cook until vermicelli is tender yet firm to the bite, 2 to 4 minutes. Drain.

Step 4
Fill a large shallow bowl with warm water.

Step 5
Dip a rice wrapper into the warm water until softened, 3 to 5 seconds. Place rice wrapper on a work surface. Let the rice paper soften for about 30 seconds. Arrange pork, a prawn half, vermicelli noodles, cilantro, spring onions, mint leaves, and romaine lettuce on the bottom third of the wrapper; roll it up halfway, tuck in the sides, and finish rolling the rest of the way. Repeat with the remaining ingredients.

NUTRITION FACTS:

328 calories; protein 19.6g; carbohydrates 56.6g; fat 2g; cholesterol 73.8mg; sodium 88.2mg

GRILLED LEMONGRASS CHICKEN

Prep:
10 mins
Cook:
10 mins
Additional:
20 mins
Total:
40 mins
Servings:
4
Yield:
4 servings

INGREDIENTS:

2 tablespoons canola oil

2 tablespoons finely chopped lemongrass

1 tablespoon lemon juice

2 teaspoons soy sauce

2 teaspoons light brown sugar

2 teaspoons minced garlic

1 teaspoon fish sauce

1 ½ pounds chicken thighs, or more to taste, pounded to an even thickness

DIRECTIONS:

Step 1
Mix canola oil, lemongrass, lemon juice, soy sauce, brown sugar, garlic, and fish sauce together in a mixing bowl until the sugar is dissolved; add chicken and turn to coat in the marinade.

Step 2
Marinate chicken in the refrigerator for 20 minutes to 1 hour.

Step 3
Preheat grill for medium heat and lightly oil the grate.

Step 4
Remove chicken thighs from the marinade and shake to remove excess marinade. Discard the remaining marinade.

Step 5
Grill chicken until no longer pink in the center and the juices run clear, 3 to 5 minutes per side. An instant-read thermometer inserted into the center should read at least 165 degrees F (74 degrees C).

NUTRITION FACTS:

308 calories; protein 29g; carbohydrates 3.9g; fat 19g; cholesterol 105mg; sodium 338.9mg.

VEGETARIAN CURRY SOUP

Prep:
30 mins
Cook:
1 hr 30 mins
Total:
1 hr 60 mins
Servings:
8
Yield:
8 servings

INGREDIENTS:

2 tablespoons vegetable oil

1 onion, coarsely chopped

2 shallots, thinly sliced

2 cloves garlic, chopped

2 inch piece fresh ginger root, thinly sliced

1 stalk lemon grass, cut into 2 inch pieces

4 tablespoons curry powder

1 green bell pepper, coarsely chopped

2 carrots, peeled and diagonally sliced

8 mushrooms, sliced

1 pound fried tofu, cut into bite-size pieces

4 cups vegetable broth

4 cups water

2 tablespoons vegetarian fish sauce (Optional)

2 teaspoons red pepper flakes

1 bay leaf
2 kaffir lime leaves
8 small potatoes, quartered
1 (14 ounce) can coconut milk
2 cups fresh bean sprouts, for garnish
8 sprigs fresh chopped cilantro, for garnish

DIRECTIONS:

Step 1
Heat oil in a large stock pot over medium heat. Saute onion and shallots until soft and translucent. Stir in garlic, ginger, lemon grass and curry powder. Cook for about 5 minutes, to release the flavors of the curry. Stir in green pepper, carrots, mushrooms and tofu. Pour in vegetable stock and water. Season with fish sauce and red pepper flakes. Bring to a boil, then stir in potatoes and coconut milk. When soup returns to a boil, reduce heat and simmer for 40 to 60 minutes, or until potatoes are tender. Garnish each bowl with a pile of bean sprouts and cilantro.

NUTRITION FACTS:

479 calories; protein 16.4g; carbohydrates 51.4g; fat 26.5g; sodium 270.9mg.

LA SA GA SOUP

Prep:
20 mins
Cook:
20 mins
Total:
40 mins
Servings:
10
Yield:
10 servings

INGREDIENTS:

3 tablespoons peanut oil

1 cup diced onion

3 tablespoons minced garlic

1 cup coconut milk, divided

1 tablespoon red curry paste, or more to taste

2 cooked chicken breast halves, shredded

8 cups chicken stock

6 tablespoons soy sauce, or to taste

¼ cup fish sauce, or to taste

1 ½ pounds angel hair pasta

¼ cup chopped fresh basil, or to taste

DIRECTIONS:

Step 1
Heat oil in a large stockpot over medium heat; saute onion and garlic until onion is tender, about 4 minutes. Add 1/2 cup coconut milk and stir continuously for 2 minutes. Stir curry paste into onion mixture until smooth, about 2 minutes.

Step 2
Pour chicken stock into onion mixture and increase heat to medium-high; cook until simmering, 3 to 4 minutes. Add soy sauce, fish sauce, and remaining 1/2 cup coconut milk; cook until heated through, 2 to 3 minutes. Add angel hair pasta, cover pot with lid, and cook until pasta is tender yet firm to the bite, about 10 minutes. Stir basil into soup.

NUTRITION FACTS:

333 calories; protein 15.1g; carbohydrates 41.8g; fat 13.5g; cholesterol 14.8mg; sodium 1709.9mg.

SHRIMP SOUP

Prep:
15 mins
Cook:
20 mins
Total:
35 mins
Servings:
6
Yield:
6 servings

INGREDIENTS:

1 tablespoon vegetable oil
2 teaspoons minced fresh garlic
2 teaspoons minced fresh ginger root
1 (10 ounce) package frozen chopped spinach, thawed and drained
salt and black pepper to taste
2 quarts chicken stock
1 cup shrimp stock
1 teaspoon hot pepper sauce (Optional)
1 teaspoon hoisin sauce (Optional)
20 peeled and deveined medium shrimp
1 (6.75 ounce) package long rice noodles (rice vermicelli)
2 green onions, chopped (Optional)

DIRECTIONS:

Step 1

Heat the vegetable oil in a large pot over medium heat. Stir in the garlic and ginger; cook and stir 1 minute. Add the spinach and season with salt and pepper. Cover, and cook until the spinach is hot, about 3 minutes. Pour in the chicken stock, shrimp stock, hot pepper sauce, and hoisin sauce. Recover, and bring to a simmer over medium-high heat.

Step 2

Once the soup reaches a simmer, stir in the shrimp and noodles. Cover, and cook 4 minutes, then stir in the green onions, and cook 5 minutes more. Season to taste with salt and pepper before serving.

NUTRITION FACTS:

212 calories; protein 14.4g; carbohydrates 28.6g; fat 4.7g; cholesterol 51.7mg; sodium 1156.2mg.

PORK CHOPS

Prep:
15 mins
Cook:
10 mins
Additional:
8 hrs
Total:
8 hrs 25 mins

INGREDIENTS:

2 tablespoons brown sugar

2 tablespoons honey

2 tablespoons fish sauce

3 tablespoons vegetable oil

2 tablespoons soy sauce

½ teaspoon Worcestershire sauce

½ teaspoon minced fresh ginger root

1 teaspoon Chinese five-spice powder

1 teaspoon sesame oil

1 teaspoon minced shallot

6 cloves garlic, minced

½ onion, chopped

2 lemon grass, chopped

¼ teaspoon salt

½ teaspoon ground black pepper

6 thin, boneless center-cut pork chops

¼ cup vegetable oil

DIRECTIONS:

Step 1

Whisk together the brown sugar, honey, fish sauce, 3 tablespoons of vegetable oil, soy sauce, Worcestershire sauce, ginger, five-spice powder, sesame oil, shallot, garlic, onion, lemon grass, salt, and pepper in a bowl, and pour into a resealable plastic bag. Add the pork chops, coat with the marinade, squeeze out excess air, and seal the bag. Marinate in the refrigerator for 8 hours.

Step 2

Heat 1/4 cup of vegetable oil in a large skillet over medium-high heat or preheat an outdoor grill for medium-high heat, and lightly oil the grate. Cook until the pork chops are no longer pink in the center, about 4 minutes on each side.

NUTRITION FACTS:

416 calories; protein 24.5g; carbohydrates 15g; fat 28.8g; cholesterol 63.1mg; sodium 814.4mg

SPRING ROLLS WITH DIPPING SAUCE

Prep:
20 mins
Cook:
5 mins
Additional:
1 hr
Total:
1 hr 25 mins
Servings:
4

INGREDIENTS:

¼ cup white vinegar

¼ cup fish sauce

2 tablespoons white sugar

2 tablespoons lime juice

1 clove garlic, minced

¼ teaspoon red pepper flakes

2 ounces rice vermicelli

8 large shrimp, peeled and deveined

4 rice wrappers (8.5 inch diameter)

2 leaves lettuce, chopped

3 tablespoons finely chopped fresh mint leaves

3 tablespoons finely chopped cilantro

4 teaspoons finely chopped Thai basil

DIRECTIONS:

Step 1
Whisk vinegar, fish sauce, sugar, lime juice, garlic, and red pepper flakes together in a small bowl. Set the dipping sauce aside.

Step 2
Fill a large bowl with room temperature water. Add rice vermicelli and soak for 1 hour.

Step 3
Bring a large pot of water to a boil. Drop in shrimp and cook until curled and pink, about 1 minute. Remove the shrimp and drain. Slice each shrimp in half lengthwise. Transfer rice vermicelli noodles to the pot of boiling water and cook for 1 minute. Remove and drain in a colander. Immediately rinse the vermicelli with cold water, stirring to separate the noodles.

Step 4
To assemble the rolls, dip 1 rice wrapper in a large bowl of room temperature water for a few seconds to soften. Place wrapper on a work surface and top with 4 shrimp halves, 1/4 of the chopped lettuce, 1/2 ounce vermicelli, and 1/4 each of the mint, cilantro, and Thai basil. Fold right and left edges of the wrapper over the ends of the filling and roll up the spring roll. Repeat with remaining wrappers and ingredients. Cut each roll in half and serve with dipping sauce.

NUTRITION FACTS:

137 calories; protein 10.1g; carbohydrates 22.5g; fat 0.7g; cholesterol 63.9mg; sodium 1170.4mg.

SPRING ROLL PIZZA

Prep:
20 mins
Cook:
20 mins
Total:
40 mins
Servings:
8
Yield:
2 pizzas

INGREDIENTS:

1 (12 ounce) package CAULIPOWER® Cauliflower Pizza Crusts
6 ounces broccoli coleslaw mix
3 tablespoons very thinly sliced red onion
1 tablespoon olive oil
½ cup peanut sauce
⅔ cup diced cooked chicken
½ cup shredded mozzarella cheese
2 tablespoons chopped fresh basil
2 tablespoons chopped fresh cilantro
1 tablespoon chopped fresh mint

DIRECTIONS:

Step 1
Preheat the oven to 425 degrees F (220 degrees C).

Step 2
Line a baking sheet with parchment paper.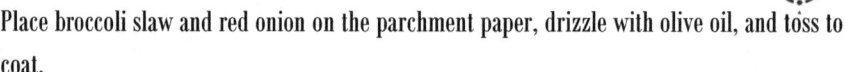
Place broccoli slaw and red onion on the parchment paper, drizzle with olive oil, and toss to coat.

Step 3
Bake for 5 minutes; remove from oven, and set aside. Leave oven on.

Step 4
Spread 1/2 of the peanut sauce on one of the pizza crusts. Top with broccoli-onion mixture, 1/2 of the chicken, and 1/2 of the mozzarella cheese. Repeat with second crust and remaining ingredients.

Step 5
Place pizzas directly on oven rack and bake until crust is golden brown, 13 to 15 minutes.

Step 6
Sprinkle basil, cilantro, and mint on each pizza before serving.

NUTRITION FACTS:

240 calories; protein 8.3g; carbohydrates 22.9g; fat 12.8g; cholesterol 24.8mg; sodium 178.6mg.

SPICY VIETNAMESE BEEF NOODLE SOUP

Prep:
20 mins
Cook:
5 hrs 15 mins
Total:
5 hrs 35 mins
Servings:
8
Yield:
8 servings

INGREDIENTS:

Broth:

1 tablespoon vegetable oil
2 thick slices beef shank
2 pounds beef oxtail, cut into pieces
1 (6 inch) piece fresh ginger, sliced
6 whole star anise
1 teaspoon fennel seed
1 teaspoon whole coriander seeds
2 whole cloves
1 cinnamon stick
1 cardamom pod

3 quarts water
1 onion, halved
6 cloves garlic
2 tablespoons white sugar
1 bay leaf
2 tablespoons fish sauce
1 tablespoon soy sauce
1 (16 ounce) package fresh rice noodles
1 cup fresh bean sprouts, or to taste
1 fresh jalapeno pepper, sliced into rings, or to taste

DIRECTIONS:

Step 1
Heat oil in a large pot over medium-high heat. Cook beef shank, oxtail pieces, and ginger in hot oil, turning occasionally, until browned, 3 to 5 minutes per side. Add star anise, fennel seed, coriander seed, cloves, cinnamon stick, and cardamom pod to the pot and saute until fragrant, about 30 seconds.

Step 2
Stir water, onion, garlic, white sugar, and bay leaf into beef mixture; bring to a boil, reduce heat to low, and simmer until broth is flavorful and meat is falling off the bone, 5 to 6 hours. Remove meat and reserve. Strain broth into a pot; discard strained spices and vegetables.

Step 3
Chop beef shank meat and add to broth in pot; stir in fish sauce and soy sauce. Brroth simmer and reduce heat to low to keep warm.

Step 4
Place rice noodles in a large bowl and cover with hot water. Set aside until noodles are softened, about 5 minutes. Drain and rinse in cold water.

Step 5

Place a handful of bean sprouts in the bottom of a large soup bowl. Top with a large handful of prepared rice noodles and drop a few jalapeno slices over noodles. Ladle beef broth into bowl to cover noodles.

NUTRITION FACTS:

390 calories; protein 30g; carbohydrates 33.9g; fat 14.5g; cholesterol 88.6mg; sodium 527.9mg.

NUOC CHAM

Prep:
5 mins
Cook:
5 mins
Additional:
1 hr
Total:
1 hr 10 mins
Servings:
10
Yield:
10 servings

INGREDIENTS:

3 ½ fluid ounces water
6 spicy red chile peppers, seeded and minced
6 cloves garlic, minced
¼ cup fish sauce
¼ cup rice vinegar
¼ cup white sugar
¼ cup lemon juice

DIRECTIONS:

Step 1
Stir water, chile peppers, garlic, fish sauce, rice vinegar, and sugar together in a saucepan over medium-low heat until sugar dissolves into the liquid; remove from heat and set aside to cool completely, about 1 hour.

Step 2
Stir lemon juice into the cooled liquid.

NUTRITION FACTS:

36 calories; protein 0.9g; carbohydrates 8.7g; fat 0.1g; sodium 440.8mg.

GOLDEN CHICKEN WINGS

Prep:
15 mins
Cook:
30 mins
Additional:
2 hrs
Total:
2 hrs 45 mins
Servings:
4
Yield:
4 servings

INGREDIENTS:

12 chicken wings, tips removed and wings cut in half at joint
2 cloves cloves garlic, peeled and coarsely chopped
½ onion, cut into chunks
¼ cup soy sauce
¼ cup Asian fish sauce
2 tablespoons fresh lemon juice
2 tablespoons sesame oil
1 teaspoon salt
1 teaspoon freshly ground black pepper
1 tablespoon garlic powder
1 tablespoon white sugar

DIRECTIONS:

Step 1
Place the chicken wings, garlic, and onion into a large bowl. Pour in soy sauce, fish sauce, lemon juice, and sesame oil. Season with salt, pepper, garlic powder, and sugar; toss together until well coated. Cover and refrigerate 2 hours to overnight.

Step 2
Preheat oven to 400 degrees F (200 degrees C). Line a 9x13 inch baking dish with aluminum foil.

Step 3
Remove wings from marinade, reserving extra. Arrange wings in a single layer over bottom of prepared dish. Bake in preheated oven, turning once and brushing with reserved marinade, until deep, golden brown and meat juices run clear, approximately 30 minutes.

NUTRITION FACTS:

716 calories; protein 53g; carbohydrates 9.1g; fat 50.9g; cholesterol 212.5mg; sodium 2780.7mg.

BANH-MI

Prep:
20 mins
Cook:
25 mins
Total:
45 mins
Servings:
2
Yield:
2 sandwiches

INGREDIENTS:

2 portobello mushroom caps, sliced
2 teaspoons olive oil
salt and pepper to taste
1 carrot, sliced into sticks
1 daikon (white) radish, sliced into sticks
1 cup rice vinegar
½ cup fresh lime juice
½ cup cold water
½ cup chilled lime juice
2 teaspoons soy sauce
1 teaspoon nuoc mam (Vietnamese fish sauce)
½ teaspoon toasted sesame oil
2 tablespoons canola oil
2 teaspoons minced garlic
⅓ cup white sugar

⅓ cup cold water
1 jalapeno pepper, thinly sliced
8 sprigs fresh cilantro with stems
1 medium cucumber, sliced into thin strips
2 sprigs fresh Thai basil
2 (7 inch) French bread baguettes, split lengthwise

DIRECTIONS:

Step 1
Preheat the oven to 450 degrees F (230 degrees C). Place the mushrooms on a baking sheet. Drizzle with a little olive oil and season with salt and pepper. Roast in the preheated oven for about 25 minutes. Cool slightly, then slice into strips.

Step 2
While the mushrooms are roasting, bring a saucepan of water to a boil. Plunge the carrot and radish sticks into the boiling water and after a few seconds, remove them and plunge them into a bowl of ice water to stop the cooking. In a separate bowl, stir together the rice vinegar, 1/2 cup of lime juice and 1/2 cup cold water. Transfer the carrot and radish to the vinegar and lime marinade and let them soak for at least 15 minutes, longer if it's convenient.

Step 3
In a small bowl, stir together the remaining lime juice, soy sauce, fish sauce, sesame oil, canola oil, 1/3 cup sugar and 1/3 cup water. This is the sandwich sauce.

Step 4
To assemble sandwiches, sprinkle a little of the sandwich sauce onto each half of the French loaves. Place the roasted mushrooms onto the bottom half of each roll and sprinkle with a little more sauce. Top with a few slices of jalapeno, a few sticks of carrot and radish (minus the marinade), cucumber, basil and cilantro. Close with the tops of the bread and serve.

NUTRITION FACTS:

760 calories; protein 19.5g; carbohydrates 128.4g; fat 22.8g; sodium 1282.3mg.

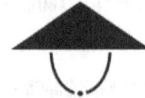

BEEF AND RED CABBAGE BOWL

Prep:
25 mins
Cook:
5 mins
Total:
30 mins
Servings:
4

INGREDIENTS:

1 head red cabbage
1 red onion, halved
3 tablespoons canola oil, divided
1 pound lean ground beef
1 red Fresno chile pepper, sliced very thinly
2 teaspoons paprika
1 teaspoon kosher salt
2 tablespoons lime juice
1 tablespoon fish sauce
1 teaspoon packed brown sugar
½ teaspoon grated lime zest
½ cup chopped fresh cilantro
¼ cup chopped fresh mint
1 lime, cut into wedges

DIRECTIONS:

Instructions Checklist

Step 1

Cut cabbage in half on a flat work surface. Empty one half of the core and most of the interior leaves to act as a bowl. Slice the other half thinly.

Step 2

Finely chop 1/2 the red onion and slice the other half thinly.

Step 3

Heat 1 tablespoon canola oil in a large skillet over medium heat. Add the chopped onion, ground beef, Fresno chile, paprika, and salt. Cook, breaking up and stirring occasionally, until beef is browned and crumbly, 5 to 7 minutes.

Step 4

Whisk remaining oil, lime juice, fish sauce, brown sugar, and lime zest together in a small bowl. Stir into the beef mixture and combine thoroughly. Scoop the heated mixture into the cabbage bowl. Top with the sliced cabbage, sliced onion, cilantro, and mint. Serve with lime wedges.

NUTRITION FACTS:

410 calories; protein 23.8g; carbohydrates 22.5g; fat 26.6g; cholesterol 68.5mg; sodium 877.9mg.

BANH XEO

Prep:
20 mins
Cook:
5 mins
Total:
25 mins
Servings:
4
Yield:
4 to 6 pancakes

INGREDIENTS:

Crepe Batter:

1 cup rice flour
½ teaspoon white sugar
½ teaspoon salt
¼ teaspoon ground turmeric
1 cup coconut milk
½ cup water

Filling:

2 tablespoons vegetable oil, divided, or as needed

2 tablespoons minced shallot

2 cloves garlic, minced, or more to taste

¾ pound fresh shrimp, peeled and deveined

2 tablespoons fish sauce, or more to taste

salt to taste

1 pound mung bean sprouts

4 lettuce leaves, or as needed

DIRECTIONS:

Step 1
Mix rice flour, sugar, 1/2 teaspoon salt, and turmeric together in a large bowl. Beat in coconut milk to make a thick batter. Slowly beat in water until batter is the consistency of a thin crepe batter.

Step 2
Heat 1 1/2 tablespoon oil in a large skillet over medium-high heat. Add shallot and garlic; cook and stir until fragrant but not browning, 1 to 2 minutes. Add shrimp; saute until cooked through and opaque, 3 to 4 minutes. Season with fish sauce and salt. Transfer filling to a bowl.

Step 3
Preheat oven to 200 degrees F (95 degrees C).

Step 4
Wipe out skillet and reheat over medium heat. Add remaining 1 1/2 teaspoon oil. Stir crepe batter and pour 1/2 cup into the hot skillet, swirling to coat the bottom. Lay 3 or 4 of the cooked shrimp on the bottom half of the crepe. Top with a small handful of bean sprouts. Cook until batter looks set and edges start to brown, about 1 minute. Fold crepe over and slide onto an oven-safe plate.

Step 5
Place crepe in the preheated oven to keep warm. Repeat with remaining batter and filling.

Step 6
Serve lettuce leaves alongside filled crepes. Break off pieces of crepe and roll up in lettuce leaves to eat.

NUTRITION FACTS:

788 calories; protein 45.2g; carbohydrates 107g; fat 21.5g; cholesterol 129.2mg; sodium 1052.7mg.

EGGPLANT WITH SPICY SAUCE

Prep:
25 mins
Cook:
11 mins
Total:
36 mins
Servings:
2
Yield:
2 servings

INGREDIENTS:

3 tablespoons vegetable oil, divided

1 white eggplant, sliced

3 tablespoons minced lemongrass

1 tablespoon crushed garlic

1 tablespoon chopped green onion

1 tablespoon chopped fresh basil

1 teaspoon minced red chile pepper

1 teaspoon minced fresh ginger

1 tablespoon oyster sauce

1 teaspoon white sugar

DIRECTIONS:

Step 1
Heat 1 tablespoon oil in a skillet over medium heat. Add eggplant; cook until golden brown and soft, but not mushy, 3 to 5 minutes per side.

Step 2
Mix remaining 2 tablespoons oil, lemongrass, garlic, green onion, basil, red chile, and ginger together in a bowl. Pour over eggplant in the skillet. Cook until green onion wilts, about 3 minutes. Stir in oyster sauce and sugar. Cook until flavors combine, 2 to 3 minutes. Remove from heat.

NUTRITION FACTS:

273 calories; protein 3.3g; carbohydrates 21.6g; fat 21.2g; sodium 62mg.

CARAMEL CHICKEN

Prep:
10 mins
Cook:
15 mins
Additional:
10 mins
Total:
35 mins
Servings:
6

INGREDIENTS:

2 tablespoons white sugar
2 tablespoons fish sauce
ground black pepper to taste
3 pounds chicken thighs

Caramel Sauce:

3 tablespoons water
1 tablespoon fish sauce
½ tablespoon white sugar
3 teaspoons rice vinegar
3 tablespoons vegetable oil, divided
5 cloves garlic, minced
2 jalapeno peppers, sliced

DIRECTIONS:

Step 1
Combine sugar, fish sauce, and black pepper in a shallow plate and turn chicken in the marinade. Set aside for 10 minutes.

Step 2
Combine water, fish sauce, sugar, and rice vinegar in a bowl. Set caramel sauce aside.

Step 3
Heat a cast-iron skillet over medium-high heat. Add 1 tablespoon oil and pan-fry chicken, skin-side up, until bottoms turn slightly crispy and brown, about 5 minutes. Turn and cook until skin is slightly charred, about 5 minutes. Remove chicken from skillet and transfer to a plate.

Step 4
Add remaining 2 tablespoons oil to the skillet and cook garlic for 30 seconds. Return chicken to the skillet and add caramel sauce. Reduce heat to a simmer and cook until chicken is no longer pink at the bone and the juices run clear. Caramel sauce should be reduced and turn amber in color. Add jalapenos and cook for 1 more minute.

NUTRITION FACTS:

464 calories; protein 38.7g; carbohydrates 6.7g; fat 30.4g;

FRESH SPRING ROLLS

Prep:

45 mins

Cook:

5 mins

Total:

50 mins

Servings:

8

Yield:

8 spring rolls

INGREDIENTS:

2 ounces rice vermicelli

8 rice wrappers (8.5 inch diameter)

8 large cooked shrimp - peeled, deveined and cut in half

1 ⅓ tablespoons chopped fresh Thai basil

3 tablespoons chopped fresh mint leaves

3 tablespoons chopped fresh cilantro

2 leaves lettuce, chopped

4 teaspoons fish sauce

¼ cup water

2 tablespoons fresh lime juice

1 clove garlic, minced

2 tablespoons white sugar

½ teaspoon garlic chili sauce

3 tablespoons hoisin sauce

1 teaspoon finely chopped peanuts

DIRECTIONS:

Step 1
Bring a medium saucepan of water to boil. Boil rice vermicelli 3 to 5 minutes, or until al dente, and drain.

Step 2
Fill a large bowl with warm water. Dip one wrapper into the hot water for 1 second to soften. Lay wrapper flat. In a row across the center, place 2 shrimp halves, a handful of vermicelli, basil, mint, cilantro and lettuce, leaving about 2 inches uncovered on each side. Fold uncovered sides inward, then tightly roll the wrapper, beginning at the end with the lettuce. Repeat with remaining ingredients.

Step 3
In a small bowl, mix the fish sauce, water, lime juice, garlic, sugar and chili sauce.

Step 4
In another small bowl, mix the hoisin sauce and peanuts.

Step 5
Serve rolled spring rolls with the fish sauce and hoisin sauce mixtures.

NUTRITION FACTS:

82 calories; protein 3.3g; carbohydrates 15.8g; fat 0.7g; cholesterol 10.8mg; sodium 305.4mg.

VIETNAMESE SALAD ROLLS

Prep:
20 mins
Cook:
5 mins
Total:
25 mins
Servings:
8
Yield:
8 salad rolls

INGREDIENTS:

1 (8 ounce) package rice vermicelli
8 ounces cooked, peeled shrimp, cut in half lengthwise
8 rice wrappers (6.5 inch diameter)
1 carrot, julienned
1 cup shredded lettuce
¼ cup chopped fresh basil
½ cup hoisin sauce
water as needed

DIRECTIONS:

Step 1
Bring a medium saucepan of water to boil. Remove from heat. Place rice vermicelli in boiling water, remove from heat, and let soak 3 to 5 minutes, until soft. Drain, and rinse with cold water.

Step 2
Fill a large bowl with hot water. Dip one rice wrapper in the hot water for 1 second to soften. Lay wrapper flat, and place desired amounts of noodles, shrimp, carrot, lettuce and basil in the center. Roll the edges of the wrapper slightly inward. Beginning at the bottom edge of wrapper, tightly wrap the ingredients. Repeat with remaining ingredients.

Step 3
In a small bowl, mix the hoisin sauce with water until desired consistency has been attained. Heat the mixture for a few seconds in the microwave.

Step 4
Serve the spring rolls with the warm dipping sauce.

NUTRITION FACTS:

187 calories; protein 11.6g; carbohydrates 31.2g; fat 1.5g; cholesterol 57.1mg; sodium 344mg.

VIETNAMESE CHICKEN SALAD

Prep:
30 mins
Total:
30 mins
Servings:
4
Yield:
4 servings

INGREDIENTS:

1 tablespoon finely chopped green chile peppers

1 tablespoon rice vinegar

2 tablespoons fresh lime juice

3 tablespoons Asian fish sauce

3 cloves garlic, minced

1 tablespoon white sugar

1 tablespoon Asian (toasted) sesame oil

2 tablespoons vegetable oil

1 teaspoon black pepper

2 cooked skinless boneless chicken breast halves, shredded

½ head cabbage, cored and thinly sliced

1 carrot, cut into matchsticks

⅓ onion, finely chopped

⅓ cup finely chopped dry roasted peanuts

⅓ cup chopped fresh cilantro

DIRECTIONS:

Step 1
Stir together the chopped green chiles, rice vinegar, lime juice, fish sauce, garlic, sugar, sesame oil, vegetable oil, and black pepper until the mixture is thoroughly combined and the sugar is dissolved.

Step 2
Place the chicken, cabbage, carrot, onion, peanuts, and cilantro in a salad bowl, and toss thoroughly together with tongs. Pour the dressing over the salad and toss again. Serve immediately.

NUTRITION FACTS:

303 calories; protein 19.2g; carbohydrates 19.3g; fat 17.9g; cholesterol 36.5mg; sodium 990.9mg.

AROMATIC LAMB CHOPS

Prep:
10 mins
Cook:
20 mins
Additional:
8 hrs
Total:
8 hrs 30 mins
Servings:
5
Yield:
5 servings

INGREDIENTS:

15 (3 ounce) lamb loin chops (1-inch thick)
2 cloves garlic, sliced
1 teaspoon garlic powder, or to taste
1 pinch chili powder
2 tablespoons white sugar
freshly ground black pepper to taste
1 tablespoon fresh lime juice
1 tablespoon soy sauce
2 tablespoons olive oil
¼ cup chopped fresh cilantro
2 lime wedges
2 lemon wedges

DIRECTIONS:

Step 1
Place the lamb chops into a roasting pan, and season evenly with the garlic, garlic powder, chili powder, sugar, salt, and pepper. Drizzle with 1 tablespoon of lime juice, soy sauce and olive oil. Cover and refrigerate overnight.

Step 2
Preheat the oven to 400 degrees F (200 degrees C). Allow the lamb to stand at room temperature while the oven preheats.

Step 3
Roast uncovered in the preheated oven to your desired degree of doneness, about 20 minutes for medium, or 30 minutes for well done. Garnish with a sprinkle of cilantro and squeeze lemon and lime juice over the top before serving.

NUTRITION FACTS:

555 calories; protein 38.6g; carbohydrates 7.4g; fat 40.4g; cholesterol 151.3mg; sodium 300.8mg.

PORK AND FIVE SPICE

Prep:
10 mins
Cook:
2 hrs 10 mins
Total:
2 hrs 20 mins
Servings:
8
Yield:
8 servings

INGREDIENTS:

4 pounds pork shoulder, cut into cubes
1 teaspoon salt
1 teaspoon ground black pepper
¼ cup olive oil
2 cloves garlic, minced
2 tablespoons brown sugar
2 tablespoons soy sauce
1 tablespoon fish sauce
1 teaspoon Chinese five-spice powder

DIRECTIONS:

Step 1
Season pork with salt and pepper.

Step 2
Heat olive oil in a large pot over medium heat; cook pork and garlic in hot oil until the pork is completely browned, 7 to 10 minutes.

Step 3
Stir brown sugar, soy sauce, fish sauce, and five-spice powder with the pork. Reduce heat to medium-low and cook mixture at a simmer, stirring occasionally, until the pork is tender enough to easily pull apart with a fork, about 2 hours.

NUTRITION FACTS:

288 calories; protein 29.5g; carbohydrates 4.4g; fat 16.4g; cholesterol 85.2mg; sodium 712.8mg.

CARAMELIZED PORK

Prep:
15 mins
Cook:
20 mins
Total:
35 mins
Servings:
4
Yield:
4 servings

INGREDIENTS:

1 tablespoon vegetable oil

1 cup white sugar

2 pounds pork spareribs, cut into 1-inch pieces

2 green onions, cut in 2-inch lengths

1 green chile pepper, chopped

1 teaspoon ground black pepper

2 shallots, finely chopped

2 cloves garlic, minced

salt to taste

1 teaspoon Asian (toasted) sesame oil

1 tablespoon green onion, thinly sliced and separated into rings

DIRECTIONS:

Step 1

Place a large heavy skillet or wok over high heat, drizzle the oil into the pan, and pour the sugar over the oil. Cook and stir constantly until the sugar dissolves and turns a light brown color. Be careful, the melted sugar is very hot. Stir in the pork, 2 green onions, chile pepper, black pepper, shallots, garlic, and salt, and toss them in the caramelized sugar until the pork turns golden brown. Drizzle the sesame oil over the pork and vegetables, reduce the heat to low, and let simmer to reduce the juices.

Step 2

When the juices have been mostly absorbed, turn the heat back up to high, and cook and stir the pork and vegetables until the sauce has thickened and coated the pork, about 5 minutes. Sprinkle with 1 tablespoon of green onion rings.

NUTRITION FACTS:

657 calories; protein 29.9g; carbohydrates 56.8g; fat 34.7g; cholesterol 119.8mg; sodium 97.9mg.

PRAWN BANH MI

rep:
20 mins
Total:
20 mins
Servings:
6
Yield:
6 servings

INGREDIENTS:

1 large carrot, peeled and shredded
1 stalk celery, chopped
2 scallions (green onions), chopped
¼ cup rice vinegar
⅓ cup chopped fresh cilantro
3 tablespoons low-fat mayonnaise
3 tablespoons low-fat plain yogurt
1 tablespoon lime juice
⅛ teaspoon cayenne pepper
3 (12 inch) French baguettes, cut into halves
1 pound frozen cooked prawns, thawed and tails removed
18 thin slices cucumber, or more to taste

DIRECTIONS:

Step 1
Combine carrot, celery, and scallions in a bowl. Pour vinegar over vegetable mixture and toss to coat; set aside to marinate.

Step 2
Stir cilantro, mayonnaise, yogurt, lime juice, and cayenne pepper together in a bowl. Spread about 2 teaspoons cilantro sauce onto bottom piece of each baguette.

Step 3
Remove vegetables from vinegar using a slotted spoon, discarding vinegar. Spoon vegetables over cilantro sauce layer on baguette pieces.

Step 4
Mix prawns in the remaining cilantro sauce and arrange 10 prawns over vegetable layer; top with cucumber slices. Place top piece of baguette over cucumber layer, creating a sandwich.

NUTRITION FACTS:

388 calories; protein 28.2g; carbohydrates 60.9g; fat 3.3g; cholesterol 148mg; sodium 885.7mg.

VIETNAMESE STIR-FRY

Prep:
30 mins
Cook:
25 mins
Additional:
2 hrs
Total:
2 hrs 55 mins
Servings:
6
Yield:
6 servings

INGREDIENTS:

¼ cup olive oil
4 cloves garlic, minced
1 (1 inch) piece fresh ginger root, minced
¼ cup fish sauce
¼ cup reduced-sodium soy sauce
1 dash sesame oil
2 pounds sirloin tip, thinly sliced
1 tablespoon vegetable oil
2 cloves garlic, minced
3 green onions, cut into 2 inch pieces
1 large onion, thinly sliced
2 cups frozen whole green beans, partially thawed
½ cup reduced-sodium beef broth

2 tablespoons lime juice
1 tablespoon chopped fresh Thai basil
1 tablespoon chopped fresh mint
1 pinch red pepper flakes, or to taste
½ teaspoon ground black pepper
¼ cup chopped fresh cilantro

DIRECTIONS:

Step 1
Whisk together the olive oil, 4 cloves of garlic, ginger, fish sauce, soy sauce, and sesame oil in a bowl, and pour into a resealable plastic bag. Add the beef sirloin tip, coat with the marinade, squeeze out excess air, and seal the bag. Marinate in the refrigerator for 2 hours. Remove the beef sirloin tip from the marinade, and shake off excess. Discard the remaining marinade.

Step 2
Heat vegetable oil in a large skillet over medium-high heat and stir in the beef. Cook and stir until the beef is evenly browned, and no longer pink. Place beef on a plate and set aside. Reduce heat to medium, adding more vegetable oil to the skillet if needed. Stir in 2 cloves of garlic, green onion, and onion; cook and stir until the onion has softened and turned translucent, about 5 minutes. Stir in green beans, beef broth, lime juice, basil, mint, red pepper flakes and pepper. Return beef sirloin to skillet and toss to combine. Remove from heat and toss in cilantro.

NUTRITION FACTS:

475 calories; protein 31.7g; carbohydrates 8.8g; fat 34.4g;

TOFU SALAD

Prep:
25 mins
Cook:
15 mins
Additional:
1 hr
Total:
1 hr 40 mins
Servings:
6
Yield:
6 servings

INGREDIENTS:

1 tablespoon vegetable oil
2 tablespoons chopped garlic
1 (14 ounce) package tofu, drained and cubed
½ cup peanuts
2 tablespoons soy sauce
2 large cucumbers, peeled and thinly sliced
½ cup Vietnamese sweet chili sauce
¼ cup lime juice
1 bunch chopped cilantro leaves

DIRECTIONS:

Step 1

Heat the vegetable oil over medium heat in a large frying pan. Cook the garlic until fragrant, about 30 seconds. Gently stir in the tofu and peanuts; cook until the tofu has lightly browned. Pour in the soy sauce, and cook, stirring frequently, until absorbed by the tofu. Remove from heat and let cool. Refrigerate for at least 1 hour.

Step 2

Toss the sliced cucumbers together with the chili sauce, lime juice, and cilantro. Gently fold in the chilled tofu.

NUTRITION FACTS:

200 calories; protein 9.5g; carbohydrates 18.4g; fat 11.7g; sodium 635.7mg.

CHA GIO

Prep:
45 mins
Cook:
5 mins
Additional:
15 mins
Total:
65 mins
Servings:
12
Yield:
2 dozen egg rolls

INGREDIENTS:

1 cup uncooked bean threads (cellophane noodles)
1 large dried shiitake mushroom
1 pound ground pork
½ pound shrimp, chopped
1 large carrot, peeled and grated
1 small shallot, minced
2 ¼ teaspoons Vietnamese fish sauce
1 ¼ teaspoons white sugar
1 ¼ teaspoons salt
1 ¼ teaspoons ground black pepper
24 egg roll wrappers
1 egg, beaten
oil for deep frying

DIRECTIONS:

Step 1
Soak vermicelli and shiitake mushroom in warm water until pliable, about 15 minutes; drain well. Mince shiitake.

Step 2
Combine vermicelli, shiitake, pork, shrimp, carrot, shallot, fish sauce, sugar, salt, and pepper in a large bowl. Toss well to break up pork and and evenly distribute filling ingredients.

Step 3
Lay 1 egg roll wrapper diagonally on a flat surface. Spread a scant 2 tablespoons of filling across the center of the wrapper. Fold bottom corner over filling, then fold in side corners to enclose filling. Brush egg on top corner of wrapper and continue rolling to seal. Make additional egg rolls in same manner.

Step 4
Heat oil in a deep-fryer, wok, or large saucepan to 350 degrees F (175 degrees C), or until a drop of water jumps on the surface.

Step 5
Fry egg rolls until golden brown, 5 to 8 minutes. Drain on paper towels or paper bags.

NUTRITION FACTS:

228 calories; protein 12g; carbohydrates 13.8g; fat 13.5g; cholesterol 68.4mg; sodium 463.8mg.

SPICY VIETNAMESE PICKLED VEGETABLES

Prep:
20 mins
Cook:
10 mins
Additional:
1 hr 30 mins
Total:
1 hr 60 mins
Servings:
10
Yield:
10 servings

INGREDIENTS:

½ pound carrots, peeled and cut into matchsticks
½ pound purple daikon radish, peeled and cut into matchsticks
½ pound English cucumber, sliced into thin rounds
2 jalapeno peppers, sliced into rings
2 cups water
1 ½ cups rice vinegar
2 tablespoons white sugar
2 teaspoons salt

DIRECTIONS:

Step 1
Inspect 2 mason jars for cracks and rings for rust, discarding any defective ones. Immerse in simmering water until vegetables are ready. Wash new, unused lids and rings in warm soapy water.

Step 2
Divide carrots, radishes, cucumbers, and jalapeno peppers evenly into the 2 clean jars.

Step 3
Combine water, vinegar, sugar, and salt in a medium saucepan. Bring to a boil and cook until sugar is dissolved, about 3 minutes. Turn off heat and let cool for 2 minutes. Pour mixture over the vegetables in the jars and let come to room temperature, about 30 minutes.

Step 4
Screw on lids and refrigerate at least 1 hour before serving.

NUTRITION FACTS:

27 calories; protein 0.7g; carbohydrates 6.3g; fat 0.1g; sodium 487mg.

KABOCHA SQUASH SOUP

Prep:
30 mins
Cook:
25 mins
Additional:
30 mins
Total:
85 mins
Servings:
8
Yield:
8 servings

INGREDIENTS:

12 dried shiitake mushrooms
1 (10.5 ounce) package bean-thread noodles, or to taste
1 kabocha squash, quartered and seeded
1 pound ground turkey
1 ½ teaspoons fish sauce, or more to taste
1 pinch ground white pepper
3 quarts water
1 quart chicken stock
1 pound shrimp
2 scallions, chopped
3 tablespoons chopped cilantro, or to taste
cracked black pepper to taste

DIRECTIONS:

Step 1
Preheat the oven to 425 degrees F (220 degrees C).

Step 2
Dice 4 of the shiitakes and halve 8 of them. Soak in hot water for 30 minutes to rehydrate. Meanwhile, soak noodles in cold water for 15 minutes.

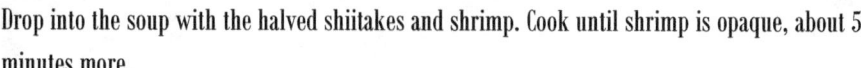

Step 3
Arrange kabocha squash on a baking pan. Add some water to the pan.

Step 4
Roast in the preheated oven until tender, about 15 minutes.

Step 5
Drain noodles and chop into small pieces. Mix noodles, diced shiitakes, turkey, fish sauce, and white pepper thoroughly using a fork. Mixing thoroughly will make the meatballs chewy and delicious.

Step 6
Bring water and chicken stock to a boil in a large stockpot. Shape turkey mixture into egg-shaped balls, or quenelles, using 2 hot, wet spoons. Drop meatballs into the boiling broth. Cook until they float, 10 to 30 seconds.

Step 7
Peel skin off the squash if desired. Dice into 1 1/2-inch pieces.
Drop into the soup with the halved shiitakes and shrimp. Cook until shrimp is opaque, about 5 minutes more.

Step 8
Taste and add more fish sauce if desired. Top with scallions, cilantro, and black pepper.

NUTRITION FACTS:

411 calories; protein 25.7g; carbohydrates 69.7g; fat 5.5g; cholesterol 128.5mg; sodium 561.2mg.

TABLE SAUCE

Prep:
10 mins
Total:
10 mins
Servings:
12

INGREDIENTS:

¼ cup lime juice
¼ cup Thai fish sauce
2 tablespoons rice vinegar
1 tablespoon white sugar
1 bird's eye chile, minced
1 clove garlic, minced

DIRECTIONS:

Step 1
Mix lime juice, fish sauce, vinegar, sugar, bird's eye chile,
and garlic together in a bowl until sugar dissolves. Serve sauce in a small bowl.

NUTRITION FACTS:

7 calories; protein 0.3g; carbohydrates 1.7g; sodium 364.9mg.

BEEF AND LETTUCE CURRY

Prep:

15 mins

Cook:

45 mins

Total:

60 mins

Servings:

4

Yield:

4 servings

INGREDIENTS:

1 cup uncooked long grain white rice

2 cups water

5 teaspoons white sugar

1 clove garlic, minced

¼ cup fish sauce

5 tablespoons water

1 ½ tablespoons chile sauce

1 lemon, juiced

2 tablespoons vegetable oil

3 cloves garlic, minced

1 pound ground beef

1 tablespoon ground cumin

1 (28 ounce) can canned diced tomatoes

2 cups lettuce leaves, torn into 1/2 inch wide strips

DIRECTIONS:

Step 1
In a pot, bring the rice and water to a boil. Reduce heat to low, cover, and simmer 25 minutes.

Step 2
In a bowl, mash together the sugar and 1 clove garlic with a pestle. Mix in the fish sauce, water, chile sauce, and lemon juice.

Step 3
Heat the oil in a wok over high heat, and quickly saute the 3 cloves garlic. Mix the beef into the wok, season with cumin, and cook until evenly brown. Pour in the tomatoes and about 1/2 the fish sauce mixture. Reduce heat to low, and simmer 20 minutes, until thickened.

Step 4
Toss the lettuce into the beef mixture. Serve at once over the cooked rice with the remaining fish sauce mixture on the side.

NUTRITION FACTS:

529 calories; protein 26.3g; carbohydrates 56.9g; fat 21g; cholesterol 69mg; sodium 1481.1mg.

CARAMEL COATED CATFISH

Prep:
15 mins
Cook:
30 mins
Total:
45 mins
Servings:
4
Yield:
4 servings

INGREDIENTS:

⅓ cup water
2 tablespoons fish sauce
2 shallots, chopped
4 cloves garlic, minced
1 ½ teaspoons ground black pepper
¼ teaspoon red pepper flakes
⅓ cup water
⅓ cup white sugar
2 pounds catfish fillets
½ teaspoon white sugar
1 tablespoon fresh lime juice
1 green onion, thinly sliced
½ cup chopped cilantro

DIRECTIONS:

Step 1
Mix 1/3 cup of water with the fish sauce in a small bowl and set aside. Combine shallots, garlic, black pepper, and red pepper flakes in a separate bowl and set aside.

Step 2
Heat 1/3 cup of water and 1/3 cup of sugar in a large skillet over medium heat, stirring occasionally until sugar turns deep golden brown. Gently stir in the fish sauce mixture and bring to a boil. Stir in the shallot mixture and cook until shallots soften, then add the catfish. Cover and cook the catfish until the fish flakes easily with a fork, about 5 minutes on each side. Place catfish on a large plate, cover, and set aside. Increase heat to high and stir in 1/2 teaspoon of sugar. Stir in the lime juice and any sauce that has collected on the plate. Bring to a boil and simmer until the sauce has reduced. Pour sauce over the catfish and garnish with green onions and cilantro.

NUTRITION FACTS:

404 calories; protein 36.8g; carbohydrates 24.1g; fat 17.4g; cholesterol 106.7mg; sodium 675.9mg.

CHICKEN AND LONG-GRAIN RICE CONGEE

Prep:
10 mins
Cook:
2 hrs
Total:
2 hrs 10 mins
Servings:
4
Yield:
4 servings

INGREDIENTS:

⅛ cup uncooked jasmine rice
1 (2.5 pound) whole chicken
3 (2 inch) pieces fresh ginger root
1 stalk lemon grass, chopped
1 tablespoon salt, or to taste
¼ cup chopped cilantro
⅛ cup chopped fresh chives
ground black pepper to taste
1 lime, cut into 8 wedges

DIRECTIONS:

Step 1
Place chicken in a stock pot. Pour in enough water to cover chicken. Add ginger, lemon grass, and salt; bring to a boil. Reduce heat, cover, and gently simmer for 1 hour to 1 1/2 hours.

Step 2
Strain broth, and return broth to stock pot. Let chicken cool, then remove bones and skin, and tear into bite-size pieces; set aside.

Step 3
Stir rice into broth, and bring to a boil. Reduce heat to medium, and cook for 30 minutes, stirring occasionally. If necessary, adjust with water or additional salt. The congee is done, but can be left to cook an additional 45 minutes for better consistency.

Step 4
Ladle congee into bowls, and top with chicken, cilantro, chives, and pepper. Squeeze lime juice to taste.

NUTRITION FACTS:

643 calories; protein 53g; carbohydrates 9.8g; fat 42.3g; cholesterol 210mg; sodium 1943.4mg.

CAO LAU

Prep:
20 mins
Cook:
10 mins
Additional:
1 hr
Total:
1 hr 30 mins

INGREDIENTS:

2 tablespoons soy sauce

4 cloves garlic, minced, or more to taste

2 teaspoons Chinese five-spice powder

2 teaspoons white sugar

1 teaspoon paprika

¼ teaspoon chicken bouillon granules

1 ½ pounds pork tenderloin, cut into cubes

2 tablespoons vegetable oil

2 tablespoons water

2 pounds fresh thick Vietnamese-style rice noodles

2 cups bean sprouts

1 cup torn lettuce leaves

1 bunch green onions, chopped

¼ cup fresh basil leaves

¼ cup fresh cilantro leaves

¼ cup crispy chow mein noodles, or more to taste

DIRECTIONS:

Step 1
Whisk soy sauce, garlic, Chinese 5-spice, sugar, paprika, and chicken bouillon together in a large glass or ceramic bowl. Add pork cubes and toss to evenly coat. Cover the bowl with plastic wrap and marinate in the refrigerator for at least 1 hour.

Step 2
Remove pork from marinade and shake off excess. Discard remaining marinade.

Step 3
Heat oil in a large skillet or wok over medium heat. Cook and stir pork in hot oil until browned, 4 to 7 minutes. Add water; cook and stir until water evaporates and pork is cooked through, about 2 minutes more.

Step 4
Bring a large pot of water to a boil. Rinse rice noodles under cold water and gently break noodles apart. Immerse noodles in boiling water until about half tender, about 30 seconds. Add bean sprouts to the water and noodles; continue cooking until tender but still firm to the bite, about 30 seconds more. Drain.

Step 5
Combine noodles and pork mixture together in a large serving dish. Top noodles with lettuce, green onion, basil, cilantro, and crispy chow mein.

NUTRITION FACTS:

488 calories; protein 23.7g; carbohydrates 78.1g; fat 8.1g; cholesterol 49mg; sodium 373mg.

SAIGON NOODLE SALAD

Prep:
25 mins
Additional:
5 mins
Total:
30 mins
Servings:
4
Yield:
4 servings

INGREDIENTS:

Dressing:

¼ cup water, or more to taste

3 tablespoons lime juice

3 tablespoons fish sauce

3 tablespoons brown sugar, or more to taste

1 clove garlic, minced

1 teaspoon minced fresh ginger root

½ teaspoon Sriracha chile sauce

Salad:

1 (8 ounce) package (linguine-width) rice noodles
2 cups thinly sliced Napa (Chinese) cabbage
1 ½ cups matchstick-cut carrots
8 ounces grilled shrimp
1 cup bean sprouts
½ English cucumber, halved lengthwise and cut into thin slices
2 green onions, thinly sliced
2 ⅔ tablespoons chopped fresh mint
2 ⅔ tablespoons chopped fresh cilantro
2 ⅔ tablespoons chopped fresh basil
½ cup coarsely chopped peanuts

DIRECTIONS:

tep 1
Whisk water, lime juice, fish sauce, brown sugar, garlic, ginger, and Sriracha together in a bowl until the sugar is dissolved.

Step 2
Bring a large pot of water to a full boil; remove from heat and soak rice noodles in the hot water for 1 minute. Stir to separate the noodles and continue soaking until the noodles are tender, about 3 minutes more. Drain noodles and rinse with cold water until cooled. Shake noodles in colander to drain as much water as possible.

Step 3
Mix noodles, cabbage, carrots, shrimp, bean sprouts, cucumber slices, green onions, mint, cilantro, and basil together in a large bowl. Drizzle the dressing over the salad and toss to coat. Top with chopped peanuts.

NUTRITION FACTS:

450 calories; protein 20.4g; carbohydrates 71g; fat 10.1g; cholesterol 109.2mg; sodium 1265.1mg.

CARAMELIZED PORK BELLY

Prep:
20 mins
Cook:
1 hr 13 mins
Additional:
10 mins
Total:
1 hr 43 mins
Servings:
6
Yield:
6 servings

INGREDIENTS:

2 pounds pork belly, trimmed
2 tablespoons white sugar
5 shallots, sliced
3 cloves garlic, chopped
3 tablespoons fish sauce
ground black pepper to taste
13 fluid ounces coconut water
6 hard-boiled eggs, peeled

DIRECTIONS:

Instructions Checklist

Step 1

Slice pork belly into 1-inch pieces layered with skin, fat, and meat.

Step 2

Heat sugar in a large wok or pot over medium heat until it melts and caramelizes into a light brown syrup, about 5 minutes. Add pork and increase heat to high. Cook and stir to render some of the pork fat, 3 to 5 minutes.

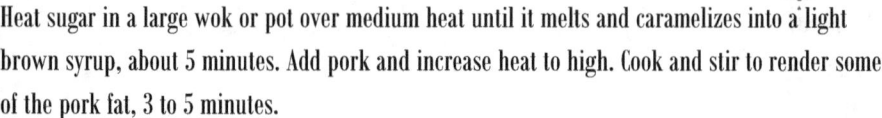

Step 3

Stir shallots and garlic into the wok. Add fish sauce and black pepper; stir to evenly coat pork. Pour in coconut water and bring to a boil. Add eggs, reduce heat to low, and simmer, covered, until pork is tender, about 1 hour.

Step 4

Remove wok from the heat and let stand, about 10 minutes. Skim the fat from the surface of the dish.

NUTRITION FACTS:

410 calories; protein 26.7g; carbohydrates 15.6g; fat 26.3g; cholesterol 266.8mg; sodium 1831.6mg.

BRAISED GREEN BEANS WITH FRIED TOFU

Prep:
20 mins
Cook:
20 mins
Total:
40 mins

INGREDIENTS:

2 tablespoons white sugar
3 tablespoons soy sauce
1 cup dry white wine
½ cup chicken broth
1 (14 ounce) package tofu, drained
salt and pepper to taste
1 tablespoon cornstarch
3 cups oil for frying, or as needed
1 onion, chopped
4 plum tomatoes, sliced into thin wedges
12 ounces fresh green beans, trimmed and cut into 3 inch pieces
1 cup bamboo shoots, drained and sliced
1 cup chicken broth, or as needed
2 tablespoons cornstarch
3 tablespoons water

DIRECTIONS:

Step 1

In a small bowl, stir together the white sugar, soy sauce, white wine and 1/2 cup of chicken broth. Set the sauce aside.

Step 2

Pat the tofu dry with paper towels, and cut into cubes. Season the cubes with salt and pepper. Sprinkle 1 tablespoon of cornstarch over them on all sides.

Step 3

Heat a little more than 1 inch of oil in a large deep skillet over medium-high heat. If you have a deep-fryer, fill to the recommended level, and heat the oil to 375 degrees F (190 degrees C). When the oil is hot, add the tofu, and fry until golden brown on all sides. Turn occasionally. Remove from the oil with a slotted spoon, and drain on paper towels.

Step 4

In a separate skillet, heat one tablespoon of oil over medium-high heat. Add the onions and green beans; cook and stir for 3 to 5 minutes. Season with salt and pepper. Stir in the tomatoes, and cook until they begin to break apart, about 4 minutes. Add the bamboo shoots, and stir to blend.

Step 5

Stir the sauce into the skillet with the beans, and bring to a boil. Cook for 5 minutes, stirring occasionally. If the liquid starts to evaporate too much, stir in up to 1 cup of chicken broth.

Step 6

Mix together the remaining 2 tablespoons of cornstarch and water until cornstarch is dissolved. Stir this into the sauce in the skillet. Simmer, stirring gently, until the sauce clears and thickens. Add the fried tofu, and stir to coat with the sauce.

NUTRITION FACTS:

380 calories; protein 11.7g; carbohydrates 28.2g; fat 21.6g; sodium 698.9mg.

LARB - LAOTIAN CHICKEN MINCE

Prep:
15 mins
Cook:
30 mins
Additional:
15 mins
Total:
60 mins

INGREDIENTS:

¼ cup uncooked long grain white rice

2 pounds skinless, boneless chicken thighs, cut into chunks

2 tablespoons peanut oil

4 cloves garlic, minced

2 tablespoons minced galangal

2 small red chile peppers, seeded and finely chopped

4 green onions, finely chopped

¼ cup fish sauce

1 tablespoon shrimp paste

1 tablespoon white sugar

3 tablespoons chopped fresh mint

2 tablespoons chopped fresh basil

¼ cup lime juice

DIRECTIONS:

Step 1
Preheat an oven to 350 degrees F (175 degrees C). Spread the rice onto a baking sheet.

Step 2
Bake the rice in the preheated oven until golden, about 15 minutes. Remove and allow to cool. Once cooled, grind into a fine powder with a spice grinder. Meanwhile, grind the chicken thigh meat in a food processor until finely ground; set aside.

Step 3
Heat the peanut oil in a wok or large skillet over medium heat. Stir in the garlic, galangal, chile peppers, and green onions; cook and stir until the garlic softens, about 3 minutes. Add the ground chicken thigh meat, and cook, stirring constantly to break up lumps, until the meat is no longer pink, about 5 minutes. Season with fish sauce, shrimp paste, and sugar. Reduce heat to medium-low, and simmer until the excess liquid has evaporated, about 5 minutes more. Stir in the ground rice, mint, basil, and lime juice to serve.

NUTRITION FACTS:

294 calories; protein 27.4g; carbohydrates 12.3g; fat 14.6g; cholesterol 92.8mg; sodium 811mg.

VERMICELLI NOODLE BOWL

Prep:
35 mins
Cook:
25 mins
Total:
60 mins
Servings:
2
Yield:
2 servings

INGREDIENTS:

¼ cup white vinegar

¼ cup fish sauce

2 tablespoons white sugar

2 tablespoons lime juice

1 clove garlic, minced

¼ teaspoon red pepper flakes

½ teaspoon canola oil

2 tablespoons chopped shallots

2 skewers

8 medium shrimp, with shells

1 (8 ounce) package rice vermicelli noodles

1 cup finely chopped lettuce

1 cup bean sprouts

1 English cucumber, cut into 2-inch matchsticks

¼ cup finely chopped pickled carrots

¼ cup finely chopped diakon radish
3 tablespoons chopped cilantro
3 tablespoons finely chopped Thai basil
3 tablespoons chopped fresh mint
¼ cup crushed peanuts

DIRECTIONS:

Step 1
Whisk together vinegar, fish sauce, sugar, lime juice, garlic, and red pepper flakes in small bowl. Set the sauce aside.

Step 2
Heat vegetable oil a small skillet over medium heat. Add shallots; cook and stir and softened and lightly caramelized, about 8 minutes.

Step 3
Preheat an outdoor grill for medium heat and lightly oil the grate. Skewer 4 shrimp on each skewer and grill until they turn pink and are charred on the outside, 1 to 2 minutes per side. Set aside.

Step 4
Bring a large pot of water to a boil. Add vermicelli noodles and cook until softened, 12 minutes. Drain noodles and rinse with cold water, stirring to separate the noodles.

Step 5
Assemble the vermicelli bowl by placing the cooked noodles in one
half of each serving bowl and the lettuce and bean sprouts in the other half. Top each bowl with cucumbers, carrots, daikon, cilantro, Thai basil, mint, peanuts, and the caramelized shallots. Serve with shrimp skewers on top and sauce on the side. Pour sauce over the top and toss thoroughly to coat before eating.

NUTRITION FACTS:

659 calories; protein 26.2g; carbohydrates 112.3g; fat 12.8g; cholesterol 36.1mg; sodium 2565.2mg.

SALT-AND-PEPPER SHRIMP

Prep:
20 mins
Cook:
6 mins
Total:
26 mins
Servings:
4
Yield:
4 servings

INGREDIENTS:

1 pound uncooked jumbo shrimp, in shell with heads attached
⅛ cup cornstarch, or more as needed
3 tablespoons peanut oil, divided
10 cloves garlic, pressed
¼ cup onion, minced
1 tablespoon minced ginger
3 scallions, chopped
1 ½ tablespoons minced jalapeno pepper
½ teaspoon kosher salt
½ teaspoon freshly cracked black pepper

DIRECTIONS:

Step 1
Use kitchen shears to cut long whiskers and sharp head point off of the shrimp. Place cornstarch in a bowl. Roll in cornstarch to coat lightly and evenly, brushing off excess.

Step 2
Heat 2 tablespoons peanut oil in a skillet over medium-high heat. Add shrimp and sauté until red and golden, about 2 minutes per side. Transfer shrimp to a paper towel-lined plate and wipe out skillet.

Step 3
Heat remaining peanut oil in the same skillet. Add garlic, onion, and ginger; cook and stir until fragrant and soft, about 1 minute. Add scallions, jalapeno, and coated shrimp. Cook and stir for 30 seconds while seasoning with most of the salt and pepper. Garnish with remaining salt and pepper before serving.

NUTRITION FACTS:

214 calories; protein 19.4g; carbohydrates 8.4g; fat 11.2g; cholesterol 172.6mg; sodium 442.4mg.

www.ingramcontent.com/pod-product-compliance
Lightning Source LLC
Chambersburg PA
CBHW070930080526
44589CB00013B/1468